# NORTH AMERICA

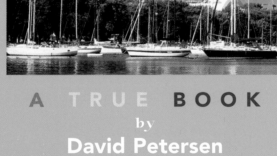

## A TRUE BOOK

by
**David Petersen**

Children's Press®

A Division of Grolier Publishing
New York  London  Hong Kong  Sydney
Danbury, Connecticut

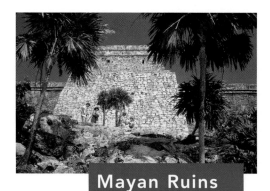

Mayan Ruins

*Reading Consultant*
**Linda Cornwell**
*Learning Resource Consultant*
*Indiana Department of*
*Education*

Visit Children's Press on the Internet at:
http://publishing.grolier.com

Library of Congress Cataloging-in-Publication Data

Petersen, David, 1946–
    North America / by David Petersen.
        p.    cm. — (A true book)
    Summary: Provides an introduction to the geography, history,
wildlife, and peoples of North America.
    ISBN: 0-516-20768-7 (lib. bdg.)        0-516-26437-0 (pbk.)
    1. North America—Juvenile literature. [1. North America.] I. Title.
II. Series.
E38.5P48      1998
970—dc21                                                           98-24337
                                                                        CIP
                                                                        AC

# Contents

The Melting Pot Continent     5

Climates and Landscapes     10

Water and Sand     19

Wild Things     27

The People of North America     34

To Find Out More     44

Important Words     46

Index     47

Meet the Author     48

Clockwise from above: Mexican ballet dancers, Little League baseball players, and an American Indian youth

# The Melting Pot Continent

North America is a land of incredible variety. The people of North America represent almost every country, race, and culture in the world. North America also features all sorts of weather—from freezing cold to hot and muggy. And it contains all kinds of land regions, from high mountains to fertile plains to dry deserts.

North and South America meet at a narrow neck of land called the Isthmus of Panama. North America includes the huge land mass north of the isthmus, plus dozens of offshore islands. It's the third largest of the earth's seven continents, covering 9,348,000 square miles (24,211,000 square kilometers).

The biggest of North America's islands, and the largest island in the world, is Greenland. It lies in the Atlantic and Arctic oceans north of Canada. Don't be fooled by Greenland's name—much of this island is covered by snow and ice throughout the year. North America's lowest temperature— -87 degrees Fahrenheit (-66 degrees Celsius)—was recorded in Greenland in 1954 at a place accurately named Northice.

North America's twenty-three independent nations include

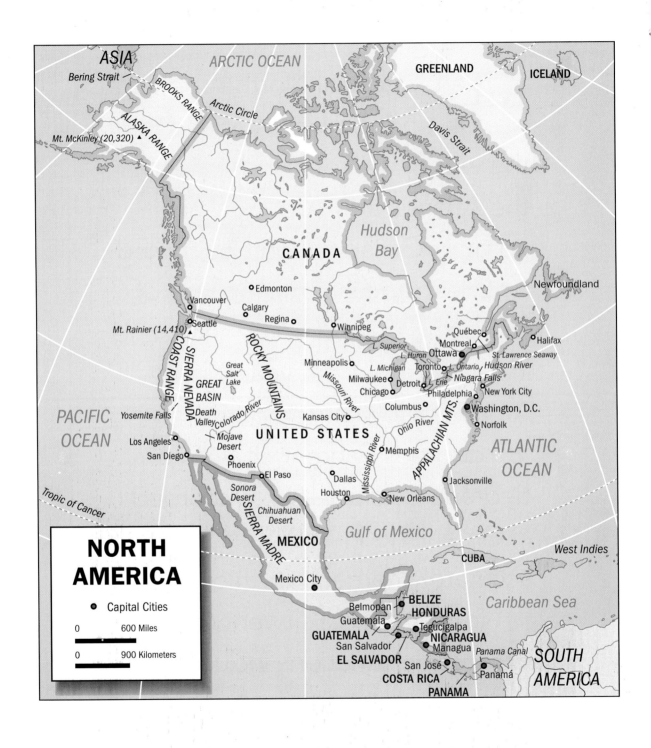

ASIA
*Bering Strait*
*ARCTIC OCEAN*
GREENLAND
ICELAND
BROOKS RANGE
*Arctic Circle*
ALASKA RANGE
▲ Mt. McKinley (20,320)
*Davis Strait*

*Hudson Bay*

CANADA

Newfoundland

● Edmonton
Vancouver
● Calgary
●Seattle
● Regina
▲ Mt. Rainier (14,410)
● Winnipeg
●Québec
Montreal ●
Halifax
*St. Lawrence Seaway*
Ottawa ●
*L. Superior*
*Hudson River*
Minneapolis
*L. Huron*
Toronto ●
●Milwaukee
*L. Michigan*
Detroit
*L. Ontario*
*Niagara Falls*
ROCKY MOUNTAINS
*Missouri River*
Chicago ●
*L. Erie*
Philadelphia ●
New York City
Great Salt Lake
GREAT BASIN
Columbus ●
● Washington, D.C.
COAST RANGE
SIERRA NEVADA
*Yosemite Falls*
*Death Valley*
*Colorado River*
Kansas City ●
*Ohio River*
● Norfolk
APPALACHIAN MTS.
*PACIFIC OCEAN*
UNITED STATES
Mojave Desert
Memphis ●
*ATLANTIC OCEAN*
Los Angeles ●
Phoenix
San Diego ●
El Paso ●
Dallas ●
*Mississippi River*
Jacksonville ●
Houston ●
*Sonora Desert*
New Orleans ●
*Tropic of Cancer*
SIERRA MADRE
*Chihuahuan Desert*
MEXICO
*Gulf of Mexico*
CUBA
*West Indies*
● Mexico City
*Caribbean Sea*
BELIZE
Belmopan ●
HONDURAS
Guatemala ●
Tegucigalpa ●
GUATEMALA
San Salvador ●
NICARAGUA
Managua ●
EL SALVADOR
*Panama Canal*
San José ●
SOUTH AMERICA
COSTA RICA
● Panamá
PANAMA

## NORTH AMERICA

● Capital Cities

0        600 Miles

0        900 Kilometers

Canada, the United States, Mexico, seven small countries south of Mexico in Central America, and thirteen island nations. The largest country on the continent is Canada, with an area of almost 4,000,000 square miles (10,000,000 sq. km). The United States is the largest in population, with more than 264 million people.

# Climates and Landscapes

This massive continent has many different climates. The northern areas of the continent tend to be colder because they receive less direct sunlight than in the south.

The northern extremes of North America—in Alaska, Canada, and Greenland—lie

The average temperature at Anchorage, Alaska, ranges from -36°F (-38°C) in winter to 86°F (30°C) in summer.

within the Arctic Circle. Up near the North Pole, summers are short and cool. Winters are long and bitterly cold. Much of the land is buried under deep snow and ice.

In the southern parts of the continent, near the equator,

The warm climate of the Bahamas draws thousands of tourists to its sandy beaches every year.

southern Mexico, Central America, and the Caribbean Islands have long, hot summers. Winters there are short and mild. Most of the continent between the frozen north and the tropical south enjoys a temperate climate, with four distinct seasons.

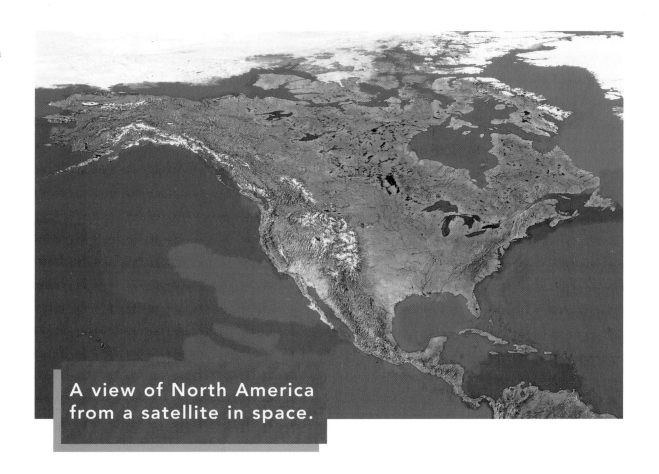

A view of North America from a satellite in space.

North America has three major geographical regions: the Western Highlands, the Eastern Highlands, and the Interior Plains.

The craggy mountains of the Western Highlands extend from Alaska south to Mexico. Major mountain ranges of the Western Highlands include the Alaska

The Rocky Mountains are 3,200 miles (5,100 kilometers) long and vary from 100 to 400 miles (160 to 640 km) wide.

Range, the Coast Range, the Rocky Mountains, and the Sierra Nevada.

The Rockies are North America's longest mountain range. These mountains stretch from Alaska to New Mexico. They form the Continental Divide. East of the divide, all rivers flow east to the Arctic Ocean, the Atlantic Ocean, or the Gulf of Mexico. West of the divide, all rivers flow west toward the Pacific Ocean.

Mount McKinley is known to the American Indians as Denali ("the Great One") but was renamed in 1896 for United States president-elect William McKinley.

The continent's highest peak is in the Alaska Range. There, in Denali National Park, Mount McKinley towers 20,320 feet (6,194 meters) above sea level.

Near the Atlantic coast, the continent rises again in the Eastern Highlands. These ancient mountains—the Appalachians—have become low and rounded over millions of years. The Appalachian Range begins in Canada and extends south to Alabama.

Between the Rocky Mountains and the Appalachians stretch the gently rolling Interior Plains, often called the "breadbasket of America."

A farm in Pennsylvania's Dutch country

Farms in these vast prairies grow wheat, corn, and other cereals and grains. The crops of the Interior Plains feed not only North America, but also much of the world.

# Water and Sand

North America's Mississippi River runs from north to south, across the Interior Plains.

Beginning in northern Minnesota near the Canadian border, the Mississippi River flows through the American heartland to the Gulf of Mexico. The Missouri River,

The Mississippi River is the longest river in the United States.

which begins in Montana, joins the Mississippi from the northwest. The Ohio River travels to the Mississippi all the way from Pennsylvania in the east. Including its tributaries (rivers that flow into it), the Mississippi runs 4,700 miles (7,600 km).

North America's largest lake is also the world's largest fresh-water lake—Lake Superior. This huge lake lies on the border between the Canadian province

The wintry shores of Lake Superior, Minnesota

of Ontario, and the U.S. states of Minnesota and Michigan.

Lake Superior is one of the five Great Lakes. The others are Huron, Ontario, Michigan, and Erie. Lake Michigan lies entirely within the United States. The other four are shared by the United States and Canada.

Until 1998, Lake Champlain was considered just another large body of water, flowing through parts of New York, Vermont, and Canada. In 1998,

President Bill Clinton signed a bill into law declaring Lake Champlain the sixth Great Lake. Many people thought Lake Champlain was too small to be considered a Great Lake. Eighteen days after the bill was signed, the President and Congress reversed their decision.

North America's most famous waterfall is Niagara Falls between Lake Erie and Lake Ontario. The continent's highest waterfall is Yosemite

Yosemite Falls is the highest waterfall in North America.

Falls, in Yosemite National Park, California. Here, the thundering waters of the Yosemite River plunge 2,425 feet (739 m) over a cliff. That's nearly half a mile straight down!

Northern Mexico and the southwestern United States

hold the continent's greatest deserts. The Mojave Desert lies in southern California and Nevada. Another desert, the Great Basin, is nearby in Nevada and Utah. South of the Great Basin, in Arizona and Mexico lies the Sonoran Desert. The Chihuahuan Desert covers parts of Mexico, New Mexico, and Texas.

The hottest temperature ever recorded in North America was 134 degrees Fahrenheit (57 degrees C) in the shade, in the

The Sonoran Desert, at Organ Pipe Cactus National Monument, (left) and Death Valley National Park (above)

Mojave Desert. That was back in 1913, in what is now Death Valley National Park, California. Death Valley also features North America's lowest elevation—282 feet (86 m) below sea level.

# Wild Things

From the soaring heat of Death Valley to the frozen Arctic Circle, each part of North America has its own community of animals and plants.

The far north is home to such hardy creatures as shaggy musk oxen, walruses, seals, and polar bears, as well as the Arctic fox

Polar bears (left) and the gray wolf (right) are two of the many animals found in the northern region of North America.

and the caribou (a member of the deer family).

A few plants can survive in this harsh climate. These include mosses, algae, lichens, and some grasses.

The lichen plant is used as an ingredient in medicines and other important products.

The Interior Plains are home to three magnificent mammals found only in North America. One of these, the pronghorn, looks like a deer and is often called an antelope, but it is neither. (All true antelopes live in Africa or Asia.) The pronghorn is a North

American original with no relatives anywhere else on Earth.

The coyote is another animal found only in North America. Other continents have wild dogs, such as the dingo of Australia, but no other continent has coyotes. To hear these creatures sing in the night is a special American treat.

A third animal that lives only on the Interior Plains is the bison—commonly called the "buffalo." Until the mid-1800s, these massive, bellowing beasts

A bison can weigh between 1,698 and 4,850 pounds (770 to 2,200 kilograms).

grazed the Great Plains in the millions. Then, within a few short years, they were hunted almost to extinction. Today, small herds are kept on ranches and in national parks throughout the United States and Canada, but even now, bison remain rare.

A large variety of plant life flourishes from Canada to Mexico, including hardwood and evergreen forests, prairie grasses, marsh and swamp plants, and cactus gardens.

The tropics of southern Mexico and Central America, hop, chirp, and crawl with jungle

Tropical forest regions are home to many animals such as the howler monkey (above) and scarlet macaws (right).

creatures. These animals include monkeys, parrots and other bright beautiful birds, and America's largest cat—the jaguar.

Tropical forest regions have more kinds of trees and other plants than anywhere else in the world. They stay green through-out the year.

# The People of North America

North America's people are just as varied as its plants, its animals, and weather. The first North Americans were prehistoric Asians. About fifteen thousand years ago, these people walked across a narrow stretch of land that at one time connected Siberia in northwestern Asia to what is now Alaska.

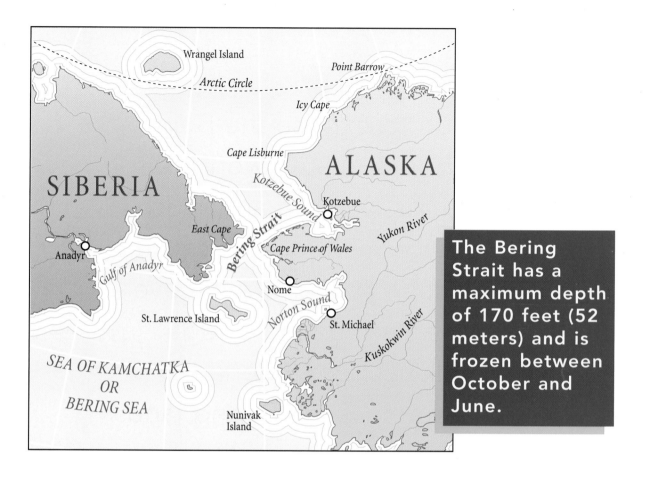

Wrangel Island
Point Barrow
Arctic Circle
Icy Cape
Cape Lisburne
ALASKA
SIBERIA
Kotzebue Sound
Kotzebue
East Cape
Bering Strait
Cape Prince of Wales
Yukon River
Anadyr
Gulf of Anadyr
Nome
Norton Sound
St. Lawrence Island
St. Michael
Kuskokwin River
SEA OF KAMCHATKA
OR
BERING SEA
Nunivak
Island

**The Bering Strait has a maximum depth of 170 feet (52 meters) and is frozen between October and June.**

That strip of land, today called the Bering land bridge, appeared during the last Ice Age, when much of the world's ocean water froze. This lowered the shallow Bering Strait

enough to expose the Bering
land bridge. Later, world temperatures warmed and much
of the ice melted. This caused
the ocean to rise, again covering the Bering land bridge.

Walking from Siberia to
Alaska across the Bering land
bridge was a hike of little
more than 50 miles (80 km).
The trip required less than a
week from Alaska. Entering
the continent this way, the first
Americans spread slowly south

The landing of Christopher
Columbus in America, 1492

and east, eventually occupying
every corner of North America.

When the European explor-
er Christopher Columbus
arrived in America in 1492, he
thought he had landed in
India, on the Asian continent.

# The First Settlers

The land belonging to the American Indians shrank, as immigrants from other countries settled in North America. The natives' homes and rights were taken away as the newcomers made their homes on Indian land. Of the original American Indian population, only a fragment remains in North America.

The few reservations that exist today continue to honor their culture, but remain in fear of losing their land.

An Indian from the Choctaw tribe performs a ceremonial dance.

When Columbus saw the dark-skinned American natives, he thought they were inhabitants of India. That's how native Americans came to be called "Indians."

Columbus told the people of Europe about the continent he had found. Soon after, many Europeans began to sail across the Atlantic Ocean to explore and live in North America. At first they came from Great Britain, Spain, and France.

Pilgrims from the *Mayflower* founded an English colony called Plymouth in 1620.

Then settlers came from other European countries. Eventually, people from all over the world sailed to North America.

Some American immigrants came in search of freedom. Others came hoping to find wealth and power. During one of the most shameful periods in human history, thousands of black Africans were brought to North America as slaves.

Today, people continue to come to North America. Among the most numerous recent immigrants are Asians—who were also the first American immigrants.

Montreal is Canada's second-largest populated city.

North America truly is a melting pot. Its variety of human races and cultures make it one of the most exciting, colorful, and diverse places in the world.

# North America Fast Facts

**Area** 9,348,000 square miles (24,211,000 sq. km)

**Coastline** 190,000 miles (30,000 km)

**Highest point** Mount McKinley (Denali), Alaska: 20,320 feet (6,194 m) above sea level

**Lowest point** Badwater, Death Valley, California: 282 feet (86 m) below sea level

**Longest river** Mississippi River

**Largest lake** Lake Superior, Canada and United States: 31,700 square miles (82,100 sq. km)

**Number of independent nations** 23

**Population** 458,000,000 (1996 estimates)

# To Find Out More

Here are some additional resources to help you learn more about the continent of North America:

 **Books**

Arvetis, Chris and Carole Palmer. **Lakes and Rivers.** Rand McNally, 1993.

Asikinack, Bill and Kate Scarborough. **Exploration into North America.** Silver Burdett Press, 1996.

Fassler, David and Kimberly Danforth. **Coming to America: The Kids' Book About Immigration.** Waterfront Books, 1992.

Sherrow, Victoria. **Endangered Mammals of North America.** H. Holt & Co., 1995.

Sorensen, Lynda. **Canada: The Land.** Rourke Books, 1995.

Thompson, Gare. **Cities: The Building of America.** Children's Press, 1997.

Wadsworth, Ginger. **Desert Discoveries.** Charlesbridge Pub., 1997.

Wormser, Richard. **American Childhoods.** Walker & Co., 1996.

# Organizations and Online Sites

## Canadian Kids Home Page
*http://www.onramp.ca/cankids/*

Created by kids for kids, this page features more than 450 links to the history and culture of Canada and its people.

## Great Lakes Homepage For Kids
*http://www.lerc.nasa.gov/WWW/k-12/Summer_Training/LincolnParkES/START_PROJECT.html*

The history of the Great Lakes designed especially for kids.

## InsectCyclopedia
*http://www.inscyclo.com/*

An encyclopedia of North American insects.

## INTELLICast: USA Weather
*http://www.intellicast.com/weather/usa*

Forecasts and weather information for North America and other countries throughout the world.

## The National Parks of the USA and Canada
*http://www.grouptravels.com/usa_can/natparks/intro.htm*

A complete listing of national and state parks, national monuments and wildlife reserves of North America.

## North America on RootsWorld
*http://www.rootsworld.com/rw/na.html*

Information about the latest in music throughout North America.

# Important Words

*continent*  one of the seven large land masses of the earth

*extinction*  a type of plant or animal that no longer exists

*immigrant*  a person who moves permanently to a new country

*mammal*  a warm-blooded animal with a backbone

*reservation*  an area of land set aside by the government for a special purpose

*strait*  a narrow strip of water that connects two larger bodies of water

*temperate*  an area that has neither very high nor very low temperatures

*tributary*  a stream or river that flows into a larger stream or river

# Index

(**Boldface** page numbers
indicate illustrations.)

Alaska, **9**, 10, **11**, 14, 15,
    34, 36
American Indians, **38**, 39
animals, 27–33, **28**, **31**,
    **33**
Appalachian Mountains,
    17
Arctic Circle, 11, 27
Arctic Ocean, 7, 15
Asians, 34, 41
Atlantic Ocean, 7, 15, 39
Bering land bridge, 35,
    36
Bering Strait, 35, **35**
Canada, 7, 9, 10, 17, 31, 32
Central America, 9, 12, 32
Chihuahuan Desert, 25
Christopher Columbus, 37,
    **37**, 39
Continental Divide, 15
Death Valley National
    Park, 26, **26**, 27
Denali National Park, 16
Eastern Highlands, 13, **13**,
    17
Great Basin, 25

Great Lakes, 22, 23
Greenland, 7, 10
Ice Age, 35
Interior Plains, 13, **13**,
    17, 18, 19, 29, 30
Isthmus of Panama, 6
Lake Champlain, 22, 23
Lake Superior, 21, **21**, 22
Mexico, 9, 12, 14, 15,
    24, 25, 32
Mississippi River, 19–21,
    **20**
Missouri River, 19
Mojave Desert, 25
Mount McKinley, 16, **16**
Niagara Falls, 23
Northice, 7
Ohio River, 20
Pacific Ocean, 15
Panama Canal, **6**
plants, 28, **29**, 32, 33, 34
Rocky Mountains, 15, 17
Sierra Nevada, 15
Sonoran Desert, 25, **26**
United States, 24, 31
    population, 9
Western Highlands, 13, **13**,
    14
Yosemite Falls, 23–24, **24**

# Meet the Author

**D**avid Petersen is the author of several books on natural history, including *Among the Elk* (Northland Publishing), and *Ghost Grizzlies* (Henry Holt). In the True Book series for Children's Press, he has written books on every continent and many national parks. David lives in Colorado with his wife, Caroline. He likes to read, write, walk in the woods, camp, hunt, fly fish, and explore the world.